# The Doctor's Poems

Ronald W. Pies MD

# Acknowledgments

The following poems first appeared in *JAMA*, which has kindly granted permission to reprint:

"The Alzheimer Sonnets" (4 poems) and "Congestive Heart Failure"

The following poems first appeared in *The Healing Muse*. Thanks to Deirdre Neilen for permission to reprint: "The Last Days of Normal" and "Lady of the Lake"

"Airport Wheelchair" first appeared in the *Comstock Review*

"Silent Spring" first appeared in *Psychiatric Times*. Thanks to Natalie Timoshin for permission to reprint. And special thanks to Dr. Steve Moffic and Dr. Rich Berlin for their encouragement.

"Utah Juniper" first appeared in the anthology, *Rough Places Plain*, ed. By M. Wizansky, Salt Marsh Pottery Press, 2005

"St. Maarten's Fire" first appeared in *Mercy of Tides*, ed. By M. Wizansky, Salt Marsh Pottery Press, 2003

The author has made every attempt to locate and credit copyright holders. Should any omissions or errors be discovered, the author will be happy to correct them. Please write to Ronald W. Pies, MD, c/o SUNY Upstate Medical University, Dept. of Psychiatry, 750 E. Adams St., Syracuse NY, 13210

# Contents


**I. The Doctor's Poems**

Dark and Bright ............................................................... 8
White-Coat Hypertension* ................................................. 10
Airport Wheelchair ........................................................... 12
Congestive Heart Failure ................................................... 14
The Alzheimer Sonnets ...................................................... 15
The Myeloma Year ............................................................ 17
The Day Before ................................................................ 17
The Last Days of Normal ................................................... 18
Buzz-cut .......................................................................... 19
Wig Shop, Beth Israel Hospital ........................................... 20
Stem Cell Transplant ........................................................ 22
Homecoming .................................................................... 23

**II. In Nature's Realm**

Utah Juniper .................................................................... 26
St. Maarten's Fire ............................................................. 28
Lady of the Lake .............................................................. 29
Silent Spring .................................................................... 31

# I. The Doctor's Poems

# Dark and Bright

Mrs. Thomas,
  my fingers curl
in your floury palm.
  You look at me
through cataracts
  and retinal bleeds;
You, who mothered
  forty broods
of jejune girls
  through Bronte and Keats,
and ended up unsightly,
  living with your daughter.
One morning,
  she slapped the oatmeal down,
and you knew
  to take your leave.

But the nurses
  aren't much better.
You squirreled their pills
  in the pouch
of your cheek,
  and almost dried away.
Perhaps the soup
  is poisoned.
Perhaps—who knows?—
  those nurses on TV
who killed their patient...

But you are safe here.
   The surgeons say
they'll pace your heart
   back to grace.
And you are well fed.
   Keats had a certain charm;
but Byron—he
   was your old true darling.


Two big tumors
   grew from your bowel
last spring;
   now your breast blooms
in kindred buds.
   Upper plates, lowers;
teeth followed eyes
   in the slow fall
that all the body knows.
You play your tapes
of Dickens
   and see bright shadows pass.
The nurse
   will tuck the sheet
about your toes.

# White-Coat Hypertension*

So many doctors,
  so many cool
smiling eyes.
  Forty years ago,
I lay in bed
  lobster-faced
and sweated out
  my heart for him,
the young Dr. Summers.
  All he said was
"Scarlatina."
  I thought
he'd scolded me
  with a nickname.


Then the boys came:
  two terms
of pressure cuffs
  and magnesium,
my blood so high
  it sang
in my ears.
  Dr. Pressler said,
"Just a little ringing,
  dear."

At fifty,
  I found the lump
myself.
  Dr. McNulty said,
"Mary, that breast
  has to go."
I still feel
  his finger scrape
across the skin
  that looked like
orange peel.


  You saunter in
   and beam down to me
your starched
  "Good morning."
You cuff me,
  pump me
and stroke your chin
  in wonder
at my shouting blood.


*The phenomenon of marked rise in blood pressure when the physician enters the examination room.

# Airport Wheelchair

—for F.P.O.

You stand
  outside the Delta terminal
as the Sky-Cap heads toward you,
  wheeling the damn thing—
just a movable frame
  of metal and leather,
but your jaw is set
  as if the Cossacks
were at your back—
  as if a push in that chair
were a shove into Hell.

After eighty years
  of raising us kids,
making a home,
  getting your degree—
and not a day
  in the clutches of doctors—
to come to *this!*

The Sky-Cap smiles
  and murmurs consolation.
You look down at the chair
  as if it bristled
with high voltage.
  At last you sit,
curling your lip

in disgust.
You look up at the Sky-Cap
  and say:
"It's just the *jewelry*, you know.
  With you around, the crooks
won't grab it."

# Congestive Heart Failure

As deaths go, it's better
  than most—
the self slipping off
  in a sea
of morphined tranquility.
  But for you, mother,
who braved Ukrainian
  pogroms,
who read us *"Do not go gentle…"*
  instead of nursery rhymes—
is this the good night
  you choose?

A porcine valve
  might save you,
but you just whistle
  through your teeth.
"Pig gristle in my heart?
  *Pffft!"*
Look, I argue,
  even God
wouldn't push kosher
  that far.
"Darling," you say,
  "This time
I fight the Cossacks
  on my own soil."

# The Alzheimer Sonnets

1.    Apple blossoms and a robin's egg sky
as I climbed higher, dizzying me,
until a fleck of bark fell in my eye.
I remember clear and sharp how that tree
shook my arms off its bearish trunk,
and sent me spinning in free fall,
clawing the air before the final clump
my leaden body made. I crawled
across the yard in league with death,
though my child's mind didn't know it.
I choked back tears and caught my breath,
biting down the pain. I wouldn't show it
then, or now, as the words spin
out from my tangled brain—if ever they were in.


2.    The barn swallows swooped low
as we made a sweaty clamor in the hay.
Our first lusting tumbled slow
and musky, morning to noon that day.
That was just before our wedding vows
and that first, unbidden birth.
If I could harvest consonants and vowels
the way I ploughed your riven earth
our first nude morning, I'd be pleased.
The doctors say I'm losing parts of me
with each plaque and tangle of disease,
but I won't feel it. I stay lanky and free

in your hay-kissed arms, where fifty years
pass in an eye-blink that knows no tears.


3.    Some nights still, I hear the horses cry
and smell the fire scorch their manes.
Death leapt up in our stallion's eye
as I tugged and wrangled with his reins.
You did your best to keep the water
coming, hose down the house,
and get our son and daughter
safe away. I ran to douse
the sparks that harried our lawn,
until, at last, the wailing engines came.
These days, my smell is nearly gone
for fruits and flowers—but old flames
still come back. With luck, I'll catch the scent
that love's blaze makes permanent.


4.    The doctors say some pinkish sludge
is what does you in. Gobs of amyloid
and twisted strands that just won't budge
from the brain. Pretty soon, a void
of neurons hangs like some old
moth-eaten sweater, where once
a solid weave of bold
thought reigned. Yet the soul hunts
for clues among the mind's gray runes,
and now and then finds some Rosetta
Stone of memory—an old Sinatra tune
that brings back spirit, if not the letter.
Love, these cells that wink out one by one
are not the song of all that we've become.

# The Myeloma Year

For Nancy

## 1. The Day Before

The day before
  had the pure blue cool
of mid-September.
  We ate Chicken Korma
at the Indian place
  as in ordinary times,
and clinked our glasses
  to luck and life.

The day before
  was a nine-elevenish day ,
crisp and cloudless,
  with fall's first red edge
bled upon the leaves.
  That smoldering
in your marrow—
  we waited for our lives
to tumble or not,
  for ashes or blue sky.

The day before
  the biopsy came back,
I said, no matter what,
  I'll always tousle your hair.
"Not if I don't have any,"

you said,
 as my heart crumbled.
 "But tonight," you added,
touching my hand,
 "I'm making your favorite—
beef stew."

# 2. The Last Days of Normal

It's just an ad
 for a large-screen TV:
a loving couple
 sitting on the couch,
the woman's long, blond hair
 caressed by—I'm guessing—
her husband
 of twenty years.
A dish of popcorn
 sits steaming
on the coffee table
 and sunlight streams
through a picture window.
 All this is normal.

In two weeks,
 we'll begin a journey
through a country
 of jagged cliffs,
whirlpools
 and volcanic springs.
You'll swallow a pill
 with the lyrical name

*lenalidomide*,
  as if Lena,
like the blond woman
  in the ad,
were a soft presence
  in our living room.
None of this is normal.
  The cells
crowding your bones
  are also
not normal.

Tonight
  we'll watch an old movie
and remember years
  when the sun
streamed in,
  so dazzling
we barely glimpsed
  the blessings of normal.


# 3. Buzz-cut


It's called "Cytoxan"
  but on fast-growing cells
it's just plain toxin:
  the cells in your mouth
I've kissed
  in salty summer;
the cells in the roots
  of your sunlit hair.

For ten days,
  you'd been spared;
but golden handfuls
  on your pillow
this week
  led finally to this:
a few deft swipes
  of cordless clippers
and the deed is done.

You smile, shrug
  and soldier on:
"There's gardening to do,"
  you say, kneeling
over April's
  first-born blooms.
Yellow crocuses
  wave in the wind,
and I am shorn
  from the inside.

# 4. Wig Shop, Beth Israel Hospital

In the wig shop
  on the 9th floor,
just above
  the Heme-Onc Clinic,
you finger the wefts
  of human hair,
deftly sewn
  into silken mesh.
Each wig tops

a mannequin's head,
its mouth frozen
  in a Mona Lisa smile.

Two ladies in waiting
  gently explain
that with a doctor's prescription,
  insurance will pay
for a "scalp prosthesis"—
  a reminder of chemo's
glum ultimatum:
  *your hair, or your life.*

Twenty years now
  you've been my wife,
and I'm ready to numb
  with heavy drink
what I try to bear.

And you?
  You are laughing
at a hat
  emblazoned
with a bald woman's face,
  proclaiming,
"My oncologist
does my hair!"

# 5. Stem Cell Transplant

If you please, Lord
  (Lord of uncertainties
who hears
  and doesn't hear)
let the stem cells
  do their work.
Let them labor
  deep in wounded marrow;
let mother cells
  build back neutrophils,
platelets
  and all the teeming life
cancer crowded out.
  Let red cells
ferry oxygen again;
  let lymphocytes
hound each virus.
  And, if you please, Lord,
let this green, April day
  be rebirth of life, leaf
and all sweet growing things
  from eternal earth.

# 6. Homecoming

Mid- May,
  and finally,
we are home.
  If we heed
the doctor's warnings,
  our antique house
is a sweet deceiver:
  mold lurks
in dark crevices,
  and spores
from tracked-in dirt
  wait to blossom
in your lungs.
  No runs to the cellar
for you: even mildew
  is villainous.

Oh—and gardening
 is out:
any turning
  of the soil
could unleash
   the treacherous
aspergillus.

We are cheerfully
 disobedient:
decked out
 in mask and gloves,

you stand
  up-wind of me,
pointing
  to black swallow-wort
invading our garden.
  I dig it out
by the roots,
  and you give me
the thumbs-up.

Love and work,
  it seems,
will outlast blight
  and the bone's burden.
I catch the light
  from your eyes
and know
  that wild blue indigo
will always flourish
  in our garden.

# II. In Nature's Realm

# Utah Juniper

We hiked today
   through Utah's canyons,
deaf to all
   but scurrying squirrels
and the crunch
   of desert soil.
Startled
   by the tortured trunk
of a Utah Juniper,
   we stopped to touch
the stiff, grey fibers—
   splayed, as if
by some blast
   within.

Yet out
   of the dun wood
sprang green leaf
   and stone-hard berry,
where death
   and life
in the brooding tree
   had married.

We learned
   how the juniper
chokes off water
   to its own branches,
and so survives

the desert drought.
The tree's core thrives;
    The inessential limbs
die out.

And you and I
    these thirty years
might have nourished
    a hundred loves,
a hundred lives—
    who knows
what stony fruit
    would have flourished?
Instead,
    we took our chances
with water
    spread
to love's essential
    branches.

# St. Maarten's Fire

In a green-blue nest
  of shoal and sea,
tucked away
  from Caribbean gale
and roiling wave,
  we snorkeled past
some fire coral,
  battering
with our flippers
  their millennial home.
With the first
  needle-burn buzz,
we thought
  we'd cut our arms
on crusted rock—
  but the blaze
drawn down our nerves
  was coral's sting:
silent, communal,
  in the end, benign—
the grave signature
  of who rules this place.

# Lady of the Lake

Our lake is warm
   in her shallows
this blue July,
   her shore a tangle
of thick milfoil.
   A mother merganser
and her chicks
   parade along the pier,
and largemouth bass
   brush against our legs.
This was where
   you couldn't swim
last year:
   after the transplant,
the lake's microbes
   were your marrow's nemesis.

A mile up the road,
   the beach is closed
by a surge
   of blue-green algae.
An official sign warns,
   "Treat every algal bloom
as a threat
   to health and life."

Thirty years now,
   you've been my wife.
Today, I watch you slice

through clear water
with Olympian strokes,
  beaming
your summer-camp smile.
  I dog-paddle behind you,
eyes peeled
  for blue-green blooms,
as I beg the lake
  for her benediction.

# Silent Spring

April, 2020

Slipping out of quarantine,
we walk hand in hand
by Dunback Meadow
into the nurturance
of pine grove
and Spring's migrant birds:
warblers, kinglets and vireos,
sweetly oblivious of virus
or the cold loneliness
of the solitary old.

Just past Clematis Brook,
we see a lone goose,
her belly pressed
against dun meadow grass.
Silent, still, bereft of mate,
she takes no notice.
But in the viral possibilities
that weigh upon us,
we take solemn note
of her.

www.ingramcontent.com/pod-product-compliance
Lightning Source LLC
Chambersburg PA
CBHW051830130726
47987CB00003B/1489